FLORIDA

A Turner Educational Services, Inc. book. Based on the Portrait
of America television series created by R.E. (Ted) Turner.

Library of Congress Number: 85-12214

1234567890 908988878685

Library of Congress Cataloging in Publication Data

Thompson, Kathleen.
Florida.

(Portrait of America)
"A Turner book."
Summary: Discusses the history, economy, culture,
and future of Florida. Also includes a state
chronology, pertinent statistics, and maps.
1. Florida—Juvenile literature. [1. Florida]
I. Title. II. Series: Thompson, Kathleen. Portrait of
America.
F311.3.T46 1985 975.9 85-12214
ISBN 0-86514-427-3 (lib. bdg.)
ISBN 0-86514-502-4 (softcover)

Cover Photo: St. Augustine Chamber of Commerce

★ ★ ★ ★ ★
Portrait of AMERICA

FLORIDA

Kathleen Thompson

Photographs from Portrait of America programs
courtesy of Turner Program Services, Inc.

A TURNER BOOK
RAINTREE PUBLISHERS

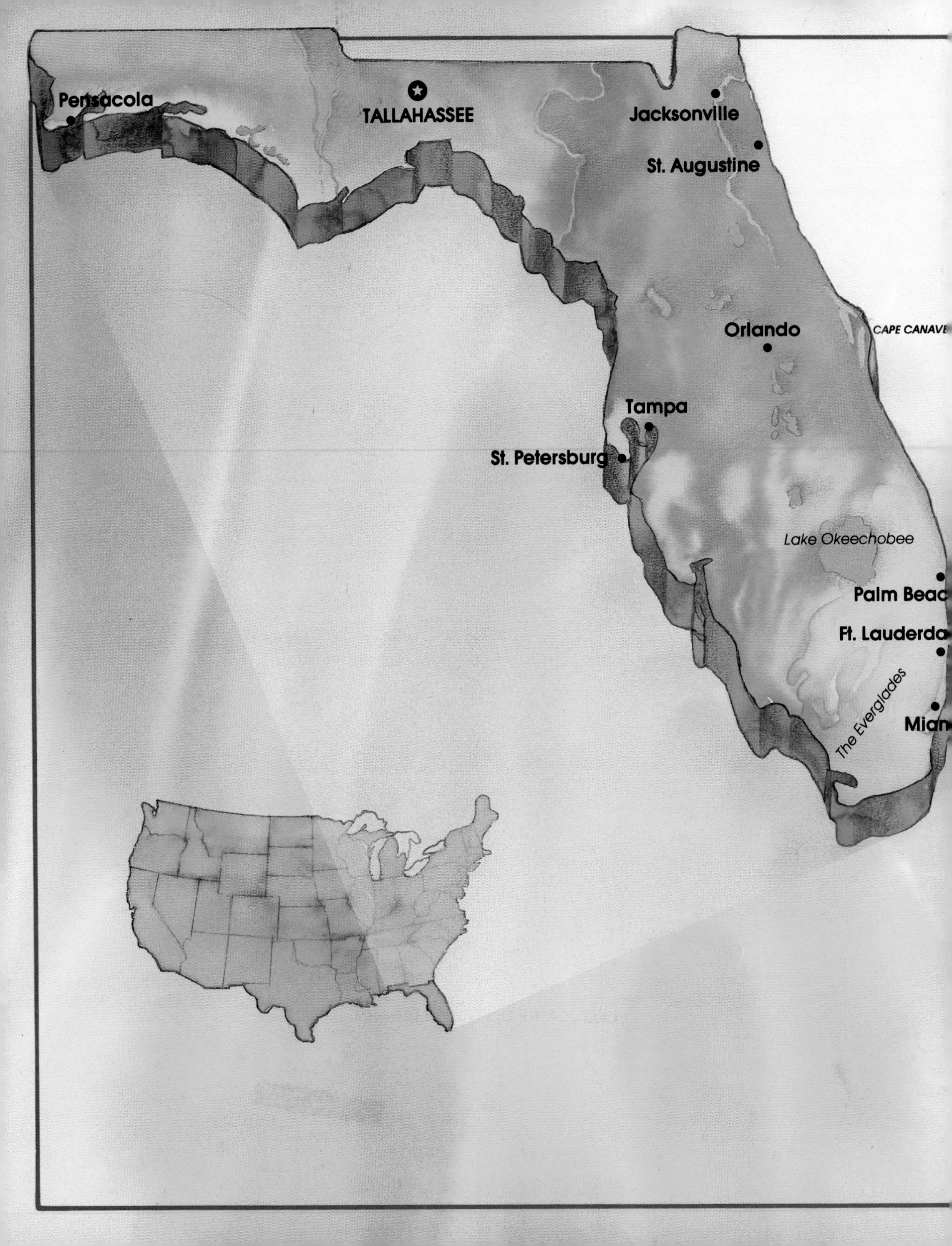
Pensacola
TALLAHASSEE
Jacksonville
St. Augustine
Orlando
Tampa
St. Petersburg
Lake Okeechobee
The Everglades

CONTENTS

SEA
DORSAY

Introduction

Florida, the Sunshine State.

The expensive shops of Palm Beach:

"When you have a customer with a last name like Ford, it is the family who are the *Fords. Or if you have Gettys, they are* the *Gettys. . . . These are the families, the old families. Palm Beach is primarily old money."*

The Cuban refugees of Miami:

"Before I came to America, I had a dream of being free and doing my art in a free land. Now I'm living it. I have it. I have my dream."

The high-tech industries:

"We're very technically oriented. We wanted to be near a university that would provide us a technical relationship. We wanted to be in an area that would be attractive in years to come so that we would be able to draw and attract good engineers."

Florida is first of all beautiful. It is a land of sunshine and smooth sand beaches. It is cypress swamps where long-legged birds ruffle their snow-white plumes.

It is next a place where tens of millions of people come to enjoy the beauty—and to threaten it.

Florida is old money, new industry, tourist traps, and the great Everglades wildlife preserve.

And all of it comes from the sun.

Boats at a dock in Key West.

THE OLDEST WOODEN
SCHOOL HOUSE IN THE U.S.

St. Augustine Chamber of Commerce

The Oldest and the Newest

There are really two histories of the United States of America. One, the more familiar of the two, begins in Jamestown and Plymouth. It is the story of English and Dutch settlement. It's the story of the thirteen colonies, the Pilgrims, and the Revolutionary War.

The other, older, one is the story of Spain. It's the conquistadors and the search for the seven cities of gold. It's Mexico, the Spanish American War and the Alamo. Most of this history belongs to the American Southwest, but it has an outpost in the east. That outpost is Florida.

Of course, there is an American history that comes before either of these. That is the history of the American Indian. And even that history puts Florida closer to Arizona and

This is the oldest schoolhouse in the United States. It was built in St. Augustine more than 200 years ago.

New Mexico than to Massachusetts and New York.

There were Indians in Florida at least 10,000 years ago, maybe more. Some of the later arrivals, like the Arawaks of the Florida Keys, probably came from South America. We believe they were short, broad-shouldered people who hunted and fished. They made their tools and dishes from shells, deer antlers, and the bones of sea animals.

When the Spanish first came to Florida, they found the Calusa and Tequesta Indians in the south, the Timucua in the central and northeast areas and the Apalachee in the northwest.

The Calusas were tall, good seamen, and fierce warriors. They defended their land and, after the Europeans came, they were pirates, attacking ships that came too close to their coast.

The search for land to farm and settle on brought the English to the new continent. The Spanish came for gold.

Rumors of gold drew Ponce de León to Florida in 1513. He may also have been looking for the fountain of youth, but those stories started long after he died. When he saw the beauty of the land he'd discovered, he called it *florida,* the Spanish word for "full of flowers." He claimed the land for Spain.

Eight years after his first visit, Ponce de León returned. This time, he planned to start a colony. But he ran into the Calusa Indians. They killed him and drove his followers away. They didn't seem to know their land had been "claimed."

In 1528, another Spanish ex-

Below is a nineteenth-century painting by George Catlin of an Osceola Indian. On the right-hand page is a nineteenth-century print of Ponce de León.

Smithsonian Institution

Florida State Archives

plorer came looking for the fabled gold. His name was Pánfilo de Narváez and he had 400 men with him. He landed near Tampa Bay and moved up the peninsula. Only four of his party survived, and he was not one of them.

In 1541, Hernando de Soto passed through Florida on his way north and discovered, not gold, but the Mississippi River. In 1559, Tristan de Luna tried to found a settlement in the Pensacola area. But the settlement failed.

Half a century after Ponce de León first set foot in Florida, the Spanish had not yet been able to gain a foothold.

So, in 1564, the French had a stab at it. A group of Huguenots—French Protestants who were trying to escape Catholic persecution in the old country—built a fortress at the base of a high bluff overlooking the St. Johns River. When the Spanish king heard about it, he got mad.

King Philip II sent Pedro Menéndez de Avilés to get rid of the French. In 1565, he entered a

Portrait of America

harbor he named in honor of St. Augustine's feast day. Then he and his men set off on an overland march to Fort Caroline. They killed the French settlers and went back to St. Augustine, where they founded the first white settlement in what is now the United States.

All of this happened almost fifty years before the first English settlement at Jamestown, in Virginia.

Monks taking an evening walk in St. Augustine.

The St. Augustine settlement survived. Menéndez established military posts where missionaries were given the job of converting the Indians to Christianity and the Spanish way of life. They had some success. They also moved up into Georgia. They went south along the lower Florida coast and west into the country where the Apalachees lived. But then the English and French began to move into the area and Spain was pushed back to the peninsula.

There were Spanish colonies all over Mexico, which then included most of the American Southwest. Spain's share of the new world was huge. But Florida was cut off from that large parcel of Spanish land. It was surrounded by the French and the English at a time when the three great world powers were almost constantly at war.

Florida was attacked by the English one year and the French the next. When those two countries went to war in America, Spain took France's side. But the English captured Cuba and, when the Seven Years' War ended, Spain traded Cuba for

St. Augustine Chamber of Commerce

Above is Matanzas Bay, in St. Augustine, with Castillo de San Marcos National Monument in the background.

Florida.

In 1763, Florida became English. It was divided into two colonies, East Florida and West Florida. They were the fourteenth and fifteenth colonies. Many British settlers moved in to raise citrus fruits and cattle, to cut timber, and to export indigo to dye English cloth.

When the Revolutionary War broke out, the fourteenth and fifteenth colonies remained loyal to England. Loyalists from the other thirteen fled south for refuge.

But the Spanish took advantage of the fact that England was busy defending its colonies to the north. During the Revolutionary War, they invaded West Florida. In 1781, England gave West Florida back to the Spanish. In 1783, the rest of Florida came back to Spain.

But Florida still suffered from

Florida Division of Tourism

Kingsley Plantation, near Fernandina Beach.

being separated from the rest of Spain's holdings in the New World. It was the only place on the southeastern part of the continent that did not belong to the United States. Settlers from the rest of the United States came into Spanish land. Some of them were runaway slaves. Some of them were Indians who had lost their own land. Some of them were simply Americans who saw unsettled land and came in to take it.

Using the runaway slaves—and Spain's inability to control the settlers—as their justification, American troops began to capture bits and pieces of Florida. In 1819, Spain finally agreed to give up their claim to the land. In return, the United States agreed to pay $5 million to American citizens for property damage. By 1821, Florida was an American territory.

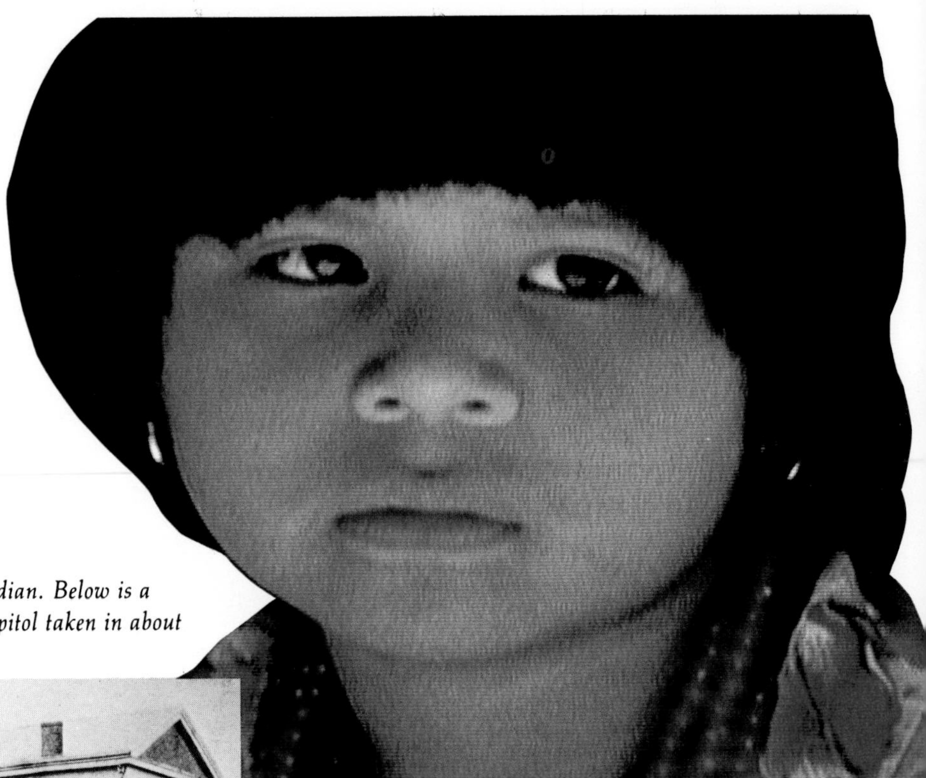

Portrait of America

At the right is a Seminole Indian. Below is a photograph of the old state capitol taken in about 1875.

Florida State Archives

Thousands of settlers poured into Florida and found that some of the best land had Indians living on it. The settlers wanted the land, so the government offered the Seminole Indians land in Oklahoma if they would leave Florida. Some, who recognized an offer they couldn't refuse, agreed to leave. Others said no. They fought for their homes. That was the beginning of the Second Seminole War. It lasted for seven years and the Seminole never surrendered. After they had been pushed back into the Everglades, where no one else wanted to live, Congress declared the war over.

Because it would be a slave state when it entered the Union,

Florida's statehood was delayed until 1845. Then, with Iowa entering as a free state a year later, Florida was admitted.

Florida's leadership at that time came from the rich plantation-owning class. They favored slavery and the Southern way of life. Only about one-third of the white families in Florida owned slaves. The rest were small farmers who cleared their own land and made their own homes. But when the Civil War began in 1860, Florida was one of the states that withdrew from the Union.

Florida was valuable to the Confederacy because of the supplies it could contribute. It sent beef, pork, and fish to the Southern troops. It was a source of sugar, syrup, fruit, potatoes, peas, and corn.

It also had a long seacoast with lots of little inlets. When ships ran the blockades that the Union had set up around the Confederacy, they could hide in these nooks along the Florida shore.

Union forces captured a lot of Florida's coastal towns early in the war. But they never captured the capital, Tallahassee. It was one of two Confederate capitals that the Union troops did not capture.

The Reconstruction Period was not as bitter in Florida as it was in many Southern states. But Florida was not readmitted to the Union until 1868 because it refused to accept some of the northern requirements.

In 1877, Florida was still very much a frontier wilderness. There were about two people per square mile, and no city in the state had a population of over 10,000. After 1880, things began to change quickly.

Valuable mineral deposits were discovered in the state. The swamplands began to be drained for farming. Huge groves of orange and lime trees were planted. And Henry M. Flagler built a railroad.

There were railroads in northern Florida when Flagler came to the state, but there was no easy way to get down to the southern beaches and the Florida Keys. Flagler built a 366-mile line that opened up what would become the resort area of the country.

By 1920, all of Florida was settled. There were over a mil-

Henry Flagler (right) was responsible for building the railroad (above) that connected the Keys with the northern part of the state. Results of the hurricane that devastated Florida in 1926 are shown below.

Florida State Archives photos

lion people living there year round. In the winter, the population swelled. People from all over the country were buying and selling Florida land as though they were playing Monopoly.

Then, in 1926, disaster struck. A severe depression hit Florida. People lost fortunes. Banks closed. And nature got into the act. Two vicious hurricanes hit, in 1926 and again in 1928, and hundreds of people were killed. As if that were not enough, the entire country went into the Great Depression of 1929.

Both the state and federal governments took strong measures to fight the depression. Things began to pick up. Then came the hurricanes of 1935 and 1941.

Most of the 800 people killed in the 1935 hurricane were WPA workers. They were veterans who had marched on Washington demanding work and had been brought to Florida to work on highway construction.

World War II brought military bases to the state. It also brought a return to prosperity. After the war, the tourist industry became the state's biggest source of income. Industry moved into the state in a big way. And Florida became a big part of the country's race into space.

In the late 1950s, Fidel Castro and his followers overthrew Cuban dictator Batista. Cuba became a Communist state and many anti-Communists fled to Florida. These Cubans have had an important impact on Florida's economy and culture.

When the Supreme Court of the United States passed its ruling against segregation in the public schools in 1954, there was trouble in Florida, as there was in many states. The Florida Constitution did not allow black and white children to go to the same schools. Integration began in 1959. By the late 1960s, most Florida schools were integrated.

Today, the tourist business continues to boom. Florida has also become a retirement center for people from all over the country. Businesses are moving into Florida because its location and climate help attract employees.

Along the beaches of southern Florida stand the newest thing in condominiums, high-rise hotels, glass and steel office buildings. But St. Augustine remains—the oldest white settlement in the country.

The New Miami

"By the end of this century, Miami will be twice the size, physically. And population-wise, close to two million. And I don't believe it. I think we'll be close to four million people by the year 2,000."

When Maurice Ferre was fifteen years old, his family moved from Puerto Rico to Miami. Since then, he's watched Miami grow. And in 1973, he became the city's mayor. It's been an exciting place to live in.

"Change has been so rapid and so drastic and so encompassing that . . . it's difficult to deal with any change, but it's difficult to deal with change that

At the left is Mayor Maurice Ferre against the background of Miami.

Portrait of America

happens over such a short period of time."

Tourists are one big reason for the growth. Another is the business drawn by Florida's attractiveness as a place to live. It shares that with other cities like Phoenix. But there's another reason for all the growth in Miami.

"Miami is a major international city and its plus is its geography. Geography makes us the entry point, both at the seaport and at the airport, of most of the traffic that goes to and from Latin America and the Caribbean. That has consequences—some good, some bad. The good is, for example, it brought us seven hundred thousand Cubans, most of them highly professional, educated, aggressive people who have become the human infrastructure, if you will, of the things that have occurred in Miami. You get the good and you get the bad. The bad is that when the economy of Venezuela is affected, the economy of Florida is affected."

Miami Convention Bureau

Miami is working hard to see that it does not become dependent on South America. It is attracting manufacturing and high-tech industries. But there are people who are left out of the business boom. As in most cities, those people are too often blacks and members of other minority groups.

"The single most important thing we desperately need in the inner ghetto in Miami is jobs. If you let people help themselves they really, most of them, will."

If Miami can find a way to spread the wealth of their new economy to those who are left out, they will have solved the biggest problem of the modern day. Maurice Ferre hopes it will happen.

"I think if there were one thing that I could change about Miami, it would be the availability for everyone to participate in the wealth and the progress and the excitement."

Portrait of America

A Day in the Sun

"I say, 'Try it. Come down for a season and spend some time away and see how much you're going to miss it—how much you're going to miss what you're leaving.' Because it's true you don't ever pick up friends like you've had

TBS

Peg Bare (left) is shown against the background of lawn bowling, one of the many activities Florida offers to retired persons.

for forty years. We had neighbors that I would like very much to have next door to me right now, and if you dwell on it, you get a little lonely. And so you don't think about it."

Peg and Ralph Bare are among the thousands of people who have moved to Florida when they retired. For many people, all over the country, Florida is *the* place to go when the kids are raised and the gold watch is handed over and the pension starts.

It's beautiful. It's sunny. There is no snow to shovel. And there is a whole culture devoted to making life after work more interesting and fulfilling.

Ralph Bare has just retired.

"Once you retire, and you do have time on your hands, you don't just stop. You still want to do things. And inactivity, I think, is the worst thing you can do."

There's a lot of activity in Florida. For the Bares, there is also family.

"We've met new people, made new friends. We have a daughter and son-in-law and two grandkids down here so it really makes it pretty nice for us."

With more high-tech industry moving into the Sun Belt, there will probably be more and more families meeting each other in Florida.

TBS

A Gold Mine of Sunlight

If you thought Florida was all tourists and orange juice . . . you're not far wrong. Oh, there's really a lot more to the state than that. There are high-tech industries and cattle, and even mines. But as far as the economy goes, tourism is number one and citrus fruits are right up there.

Tourism brings in half of Florida's income. Everything else brings in the rest. Every year, about 40 million people come to enjoy the sun and surf. While they're at it, they spend about $17 billion dollars.

For almost a hundred years, Florida has been the resort choice for the rich and famous, for the hardware store owner from Iowa, for the college student from Michigan, for the clerk from New York. It's easy to understand why.

Harvesting oranges on Key West.

Pineapples (above) and sugarcane (right) are two of Florida's important crops. The state also manufactures missiles and is the site for many space-program launchings. At the far right is a space shuttle blast-off.

Florida has the longest coastline in the United States, except for Alaska. With all its bays and inlets and islands, it has more coastline even than Texas. That means a lot of beaches. It has more coastline than California. That means a lot of sand.

It also has sun. Sunny day follows sunny day all year round. And what rain there is falls in the off season—the summer.

All that sun is good for more than lying on the beach, too. It's good for growing oranges.

Citrus fruits are an important part of both agriculture and

Florida Division of Tourism photos

manufacturing. They're the leading crop. And processing them is the leading area of manufacturing.

Altogether, manufacturing accounts for about two-thirds of the value of goods produced in Florida. Food processing ranks first.

Plants in central Florida produce orange juice and other citrus juices, canned fruit sections, and by-products. Smaller industries include the producers of orange marmalade and other jellies.

Food processing plants also

freeze, can, and package vegetables and seafood.

That's not the whole story of manufacturing in Florida, of course. The second largest area is electric machinery and equipment. Florida factories also produce transportation equipment and chemicals.

Florida also makes missiles. They make missiles for the space program and missiles for the military.

With all of this going on, it's interesting to realize that about 40 percent of the state is farm-

TBS photos

The rancher (left) and the irrigation trucks (above) attest to the fact that a large proportion of Florida is farmland.

land. Besides citrus fruits, these farms raise peanuts and pecans. They grow exotic fruits and vegetables like avocadoes, mangos, papaya, pineapples, and bananas. Florida farmers also grow melons and strawberries.

Florida's largest field crop is not soybeans or corn or wheat, but sugarcane. The cane fields of Florida are mostly near the Everglades in the Lake Okeechobee area. However, Florida does grow soybeans, about 10 million bushels a year.

Then there are the truck crops. A truck crop is grown to be taken directly to market, not to a factory for processing. Florida grows more vegetables for market than any other state except California, including celery, peppers, potatoes, corn, and snap beans.

Florida may not seem like home on the range, but a lot of cattle are raised here—beef and dairy cattle.

The mines of Florida produce phosphate, a chemical that is used in fertilizer. In fact, Florida mines about 86 percent of all the phosphate in the United States. There's also clay here, for pottery and for filtering petroleum products.

Finally, Florida produces fish. It's one of the leading commercial fishing states, specializing in shrimp and lobster.

There's a lot going on in Florida, but the state's economy is still very dependent on tourism. Tourists provided Florida's first big economic boom. They are still providing it. Florida's greatest natural resource is 93 million miles away.

They Never Surrendered

"From all the history that I can pick up from the old fellers that was here at the time when the cattle came, they claim they got the cattle out of Arizona and New Mexico and those states. They shipped the cattle down here in boxcars. Somewhere in the neighborhood of two hundred head is the way I understand it. You know, the Hereford cattle were not suited for this area here. The government does everything backward or whatever, so I'm sure that's what they done. They said, 'Send them to the Seminole. They'll either drown them or whatever.' But it so happens that the Seminole people were pretty good ranchers."

Which shouldn't surprise anybody. The Seminole people have always been good at what they chose to do—or even at what somebody else chose for them.

When new settlers—with the help of the U.S. Army—forced the Seminole off their land, they retreated to the Everglades. The war that was started to make them move to Oklahoma had lasted for seven years, and the Seminole never surrendered. Finally, Congress simply declared that the war was over. Everybody then forgot about the Seminole, except for sending them two hundred head of cattle.

Today, Florida is the second largest cattle producer in the country.

Stanlo Johns manages the thirty-four-thousand-acre Seminole cooperative ranch.

"I'm not going to say whether it's a good business for the Seminoles or not. I think—I'm sure there's other businesses they could get into and probably do, make money off of it. But then again, this is something that, you know, we're used to doing and this is all they ever

TBS

Portrait of America

At the left is Stanlo Johns, manager of a cooperative ranch that has 34,000 acres.

done all their lives till it's sort of been handed down from generation through generation. It's hard to get out of a canoe in the middle of the stream, so to speak."

The Brighton ranch is a canoe most cattle raisers wouldn't see any reason to get out of, anyway. It's a modern, successful ranch. They even make movies of the cows.

"It's much easier for us to film the cattle here and take them to the man's front door and show them to him than for the man to come down here and spend a day looking at maybe one bunch of cattle which may not consist of two hundred head."

The Seminoles have managed what few of the tribes who were displaced by whites have been able to do. They have moved into the twentieth century while they kept their people, and their values, intact.

Everglades National Park

Two Voices of Florida

Florida is a place where the world of nature meets the human world. In few places is nature more beautiful and more cherished. In few places is the human world more "worldly."

The culture of Florida constantly gives us two voices to listen to. One comes from Miami and one from the deep reeds of the Everglades. One is sophisticated, and one has a gentle simplicity. In art, there is room for both.

Two of Florida's greatest writers give us complex and interesting variations on those voices.

James Weldon Johnson was a man of the world. He was a lawyer, the first black to be admitted to the Florida bar. He was American consul to Venezuela and Nicaragua. And he

An air plant in the Everglades.

was a writer.

Johnson was famous as a poet, novelist, and lyricist. Probably his best known work was the collection of poems called *God's Trombones.* He was also famous as a man who spoke and fought for the rights of his people and all people.

Florida was there in his work.

And God stepped out on space
And He looked around and said:
I'm lonely—
I'll make me a world.

Florida State Archives

This is a photograph of writer, teacher, songwriter, and diplomat, James Weldon Johnson.

Florida State Archives

USDA Forest Service

Above is Marjorie Kinnan Rawlings, and at the left is the kind of landscape that was the setting for her novel The Yearling.

And as far as the eye of God could see
Darkness covered everything,
Blacker than a hundred midnights
Down in a cypress swamp.

Marjorie Kinnan Rawlings was born in Washington, D.C. Before she moved to Florida, she lived in a world of writers and artists, a sophisticated world. Then, in search of something she couldn't find there, she moved to a small farm in the back country of Florida. She lived almost alone there, with the herons and the deer and a small orange grove.

She wrote about nature and people who loved it. Her books were gentle and true. Her most famous book was *The Yearling,* for which she received the Pulitzer Prize in 1939. It is the poignant story of a young boy and a deer.

There are many others who have spoken from the cities and the swamps, the beaches and the backwoods of Florida. There will be many more.

Saving the Everglades

"And I like open country. I like the openness like the sea. So that always attracted me, the fact that it was not a jungle, that it was great, wonderful, open country."

Even the word Everglades has a sound of mystery to it. For the white settlers, it was always a place that frightened them, that they did not understand. But for those who did understand it—the wildlife and the Indians who were driven out of the rest of Florida—it was a refuge.

"What are the Everglades? The Everglades are the fresh water and the sawgrass. Wherever you find the sawgrass and the fresh water together, that's the Everglades."

Marjory Stoneham Douglas has known and loved the Everglades for most of her life. Author and conservationist, she wrote a book called *The Everglades: River of Grass.* It was published in 1947 and people still read it today. Mrs. Douglas was also one of the people who managed to get the Everglades declared a national park and wildlife reserve.

"(The Indians) never overkilled. They only killed enough to support life. And so they maintained the deer and other wildlife very carefully. The Indians are the original conservationists in this country."

Others were not so careful. Before the million and a half

Marjory Stoneham Douglas.

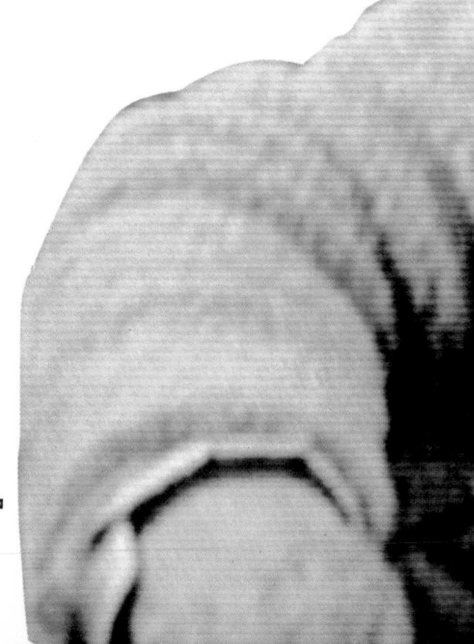

Portrait of America

TBS

acres at the tip of Florida became protected land, plume hunters used to come and kill birds by the hundreds and thousands. They sold the feathers to decorate women's hats.

Deer were hunted with packs of dogs, and a single hunter might kill up to a half dozen in one day.

Even today, the damage has not stopped.

"What they are doing to the Everglades is that they are going in with all kinds of glades buggies and, especially in the Big Cypress now, these horrible new tricycles with balloon tires. And they go off a road that's an access road for the oil people and they plunge into the Big Cypress anywhere. And where they go, they make paths. And when they make a path, they go again. And it would be difficult to get rid of those paths in under twenty years. . . . They're murdering the Big Cypress."

But Marjory Douglas keeps fighting for her beloved Everglades. She is concerned not only for their beauty, but because they are crucial as a source of water for the whole area.

"I'm sorry to be such a nuisance, but sometimes you have to be a nuisance to get attention. I use that nuisance value

Florida Division of Tourism Photos

This long view of the Everglades is flanked by two common sights there—alligators and air boats.

as cleverly as I can because, you see, I'm an old lady, and I've got all this white hair and wrinkles and everything. They can't be impolite to me."

They can be impolite to the Everglades, though. And they are. Developers dam streams that flow into the area. Tourists abuse it. Florida's economy, its population, and its popularity are growing by leaps and bounds.

Can the demands of progress be balanced with the needs of nature?

"I think the whole thing that is in question is the struggle between man's stupidity and his intelligence. And it just depends which will win. And I don't know which will win anymore than you do. But I hope that intelligence does a little better."

MICKEY'S
STREET
PARTY

Juergen Strigenz

The Future in Florida

Booms are dangerous things. The ghost towns of the West, left behind after the silver and gold mines closed, are striking evidence. The depression in Florida after the land boom of the 1920s was another clear example.

The tourist trade in Florida has lasted so long it's hard to think of it as a boom. It has a feeling of permanence to it. But the fact is, it came suddenly and it could go. Even one really bad tourist season could cause problems for the entire economy of the state. That's true of any state that depends heavily on a single industry. It's particularly true if the industry deals in a luxury, not a necessity.

But given that warning, the future of Florida looks very promising. Tourism continues to grow every year with little

Disney World, near Orlando.

The port of Miami.

sign of letting up. High-tech industries, which can choose their locations to make their employees happy, seem more and more to be building in the sun. Many of them are going to Florida. Florida's port cities are becoming more important in international trade.

It seems that the dangers in Florida's future may come from too much success, not too little. The crowds of people who come in every year demand building and development that may threaten the very things that bring them in. In Florida, the beauty of nature is valuable, not only in itself, but because it is what the state sells. In the future, it must be protected, and it is becoming more and more difficult to do that.

Miami Convention Bureau/Port of Miami

Also, those forty million tourists who come in each year mean more highways and other public facilities. That means more taxes. Right now, taxes on the goods sold to tourists are helping to support all public works in the state. But sales taxes can only get so high.

The people of Florida must walk a thin line. The future seems full of prosperity. And prosperity is the one thing Florida has to fear.

Florida Division of Tourism

Sea World, near Orlando.

Important Historical Events in Florida

1513 Spanish explorer Juan Ponce de León lands on the Florida coast in search of the legendary fountain of youth. He claims the region for Spain.

1521 Ponce de León returns to Florida to set up a colony but is wounded in an Indian battle and leaves.

1528 Pánfilo de Narváez leads a Spanish expedition to Florida's southwestern coast in search of gold.

1539 Spanish explorer Hernando de Soto lands at Tampa Bay and travels north to the Mississippi River.

1564 A group of French Protestants, called Huguenots, arrive at what is now Jacksonville and build Fort Caroline on the St. Johns River.

1565 King Philip II of Spain sends Pedro Menéndez de Avilés to drive the French out of Spanish-claimed Florida. Menéndez establishes St. Augustine, the first permanent white settlement in the United States.

1698 Fort San Carlos is built by the Spanish at Pensacola.

1702 English colonists from Carolina try unsuccessfully to take control of St. Augustine.

1740 English colonists from Georgia raid northern Florida.

1750 The Creek Indians leave Georgia and move to the Florida peninsula. They become known as the Seminole.

1762 The English capture Spanish-claimed Cuba.

1763 The Spanish give Florida to the English. Florida is divided into two colonies, East Florida and West Florida.

1768 Fifteen hundred colonists, led by Andrew Turnbull, settle at New Smyrna.

1776 Florida remains on the side of the British during the Revolutionary War. Turnbull's settlement at New Smyrna fails.

1781 The English surrender West Florida to the Spanish.

1783 Britain gives all of Florida back to Spain.

1812 A group of rebellious settlers in eastern Florida form the Republic of Florida.

1814 General Andrew Jackson leads American troops into Florida and takes Pensacola.

1819 Spain gives Florida to the United States under the terms of the Adams-Onis Treaty. The United States agrees to pay $5 million to U.S. citizens living there for property damage.

1821 The United States formally takes control of Florida.

1822 The Territory of Florida is organized by Congress. William P. DuVal is the first governor.

1835 The U.S. government tries to move the Seminole Indians to a reservation in Oklahoma. They resist and defeat Major Francis L. Dade and his troops near Bushnell, starting a seven-year war.

1845 Florida is admitted to the Union as the 27th state on March 3. The governor is William D. Moseley, and the capital is Tallahassee.

1850 Florida gets twenty-two million acres of land under the Swamp Land Act.

1861 Florida secedes from the Union to join the Confederacy.

1868 Florida is readmitted to the Union on June 25.

1884 Large phosphate deposits are found. The Kissimmee-Tampa cross-state railroad is finished.

1895 A freeze destroys most of Florida's citrus crop.

1907 Swampland near Fort Lauderdale is drained, creating some of Florida's richest farmland.

1920-1926 Land speculators flood into Florida.

1938 The Overseas Highway is opened.

1958 America's first satellite, *Explorer I*, is launched from Cape Canaveral on January 31.

1961 The United States' first manned space flight is launched from Cape Canaveral.

1969 Florida adopts a new state constitution. The first spacecraft to put men on the moon, *Apollo 11*, takes off from Cape Canaveral on July 16.

1971 Florida adopts its first income tax on corporate profits. Conservationists halt the construction of the Cross-Florida Barge Canal.

1977 The new state capitol is opened in Tallahassee.

1980 A huge wave of immigrants hits Florida's shores. Nearly 125,000 Cuban refugees arrive in the state and are eventually absorbed into the United States.

Florida Almanac

Nickname. The Sunshine State.

Capital. Tallahassee.

State Bird. Mockingbird.

State Flower. Orange blossom.

State Tree. Sabal palmetto palm.

State Motto. In God we trust.

State Song. Swanee River.

State Abbreviations. Fla. (traditional); FL (postal).

Statehood. March 3, 1845, the 27th state.

Government. Congress: U.S. senators, 2; U.S. representatives, 19. **State Legislature:** senators, 40; representatives, 120. **Counties:** 67.

Area. 58,560 sq. mi. (151,670 sq. km.), 22nd in size among the states.

Greatest Distances. north/south, 447 mi. (719 km.); east/west, 361 mi. (581 km.). **Coastline:** 580 mi. (933 km.), along the Atlantic Ocean.

Elevation. Highest: 345 ft. (105 m). **Lowest:** sea level, along the Atlantic Ocean.

Population. 1980 Census: 9,739,992 (43% increase over 1970), 7th in size among the states. **Density:** 166 persons per sq. ft. (64 persons per sq. km.). **Distribution:** 84% urban; 16% rural. **1970 Census:** 6,791,418.

Economy. Agriculture: citrus fruits, sugar cane, avocados, greenhouse products, beef cattle, hogs and pigs. **Fishing Industry:** shrimp, lobsters. **Manufacturing:** electronic and electric machinery, transportation equipment, printed material, food products, chemicals. **Mining:** phosphate rock, crushed stone.

Places to Visit

Busch Gardens in Tampa.
Cape Canaveral, near Cocoa Beach.
Cypress Gardens, near Winter Haven.
Everglades National Park, in southwestern Florida.
John Pennekamp Coral Reef State Park, near Key Largo.
Lion County Safari, near West Palm Beach.
Marineland, south of St. Augustine.
Parrot Jungle in South Miami.

Annual Events

Orange Bowl football game in Miami (New Year's Day).
Old Island Days in Key West (January-March).
Florida State Fair and Gasparilla Carnival in Tampa (February).
Festival of the States in St. Petersburg (March).
Flying High Circus in Tallahassee (May).
Firecracker 400 Auto Race in Daytona Beach (Fourth of July).
Days in Spain in St. Augustine (August).
Beaux Arts Promenade in Fort Lauderdale (November).

Florida Counties

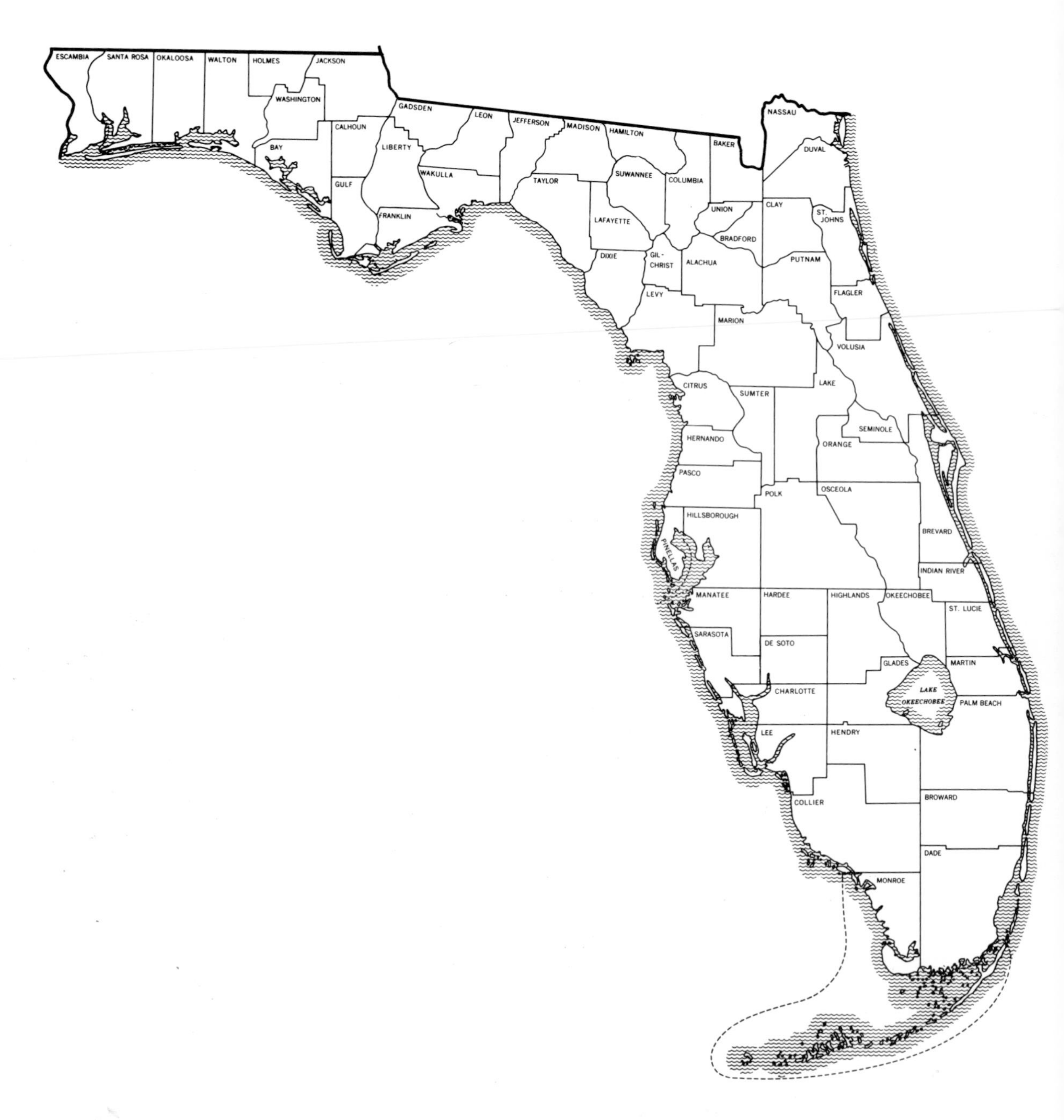